"THE LAST OF THE HUMAN FREEDOMS IS TO CHOOSE
ONE'S ATTITUDE IN ANY GIVEN SET OF CIRCUMSTANCES."

HOLOCAUST SURVIVOR, VIKTOR FRANKL

FOR MY SISTER KRISTIN,
WHOSE ULTIMATE HEALING WAS THE BEGINNING OF MY TRANSFORMATION.
~RUTH

Library of Congress Cataloging-in-Publication Data

Bachman, Ruth.
Growing through the narrow spots / written by Ruth Bachman.
p. cm.
ISBN 978-0-931674-77-8 (hardcover : alk. paper) 1. Resilience (Personality trait)
2. Adjustment (Psychology) 3. Encouragement.
4. Self-help techniques. I. Title.
BF698.35.R47B33 2012
155.2'4--dc23

2012028724

Page 1: Viktor Frankl quote reprinted with permission from Dr. Gabriele Vesely.
Page 20: Reprinted with permission from "Grace Approaching," in Breaking the
Drought: Visions of Grace by Stephen Levine, © 2007, Larson Publications.

TRISTAN Publishing, Inc.
2355 Louisiana Avenue North
Golden Valley, MN 55427

Text copyright © 2013, Ruth Bachman
Photographs copyright © 2013, Dale Bachman
ISBN 978-0-931674-77-8
First Printing
Printed in China

To learn about all of our books with a message please visit
www.TRISTANpublishing.com

To Scott

Always, with grace..

Ruth Bachman

GROWING THROUGH THE NARROW SPOTS

CHANGE IS THE RULE.
NOT THE EXCEPTION.

Change is the rule, not the exception. Small wonders happen every day; the kind we expect, like waking from sleep or the sun rising and setting; and the kind that surprise us, like a rainbow after a sudden thunderstorm. We take in these natural changes with delight and comfort, and even experience a bit of awe at their existence. But there are all the other changes that are not in the natural rhythm of life. When such a change occurs in our lives, we think we can control it, but the opposite is true.

We can only control how we respond to change. The challenge is to say "yes" and to navigate life's changes with courage and intention.

LIFE IS CHALLENGING

    Someone once told me that I make navigating change look easy. Be assured that it is not and has never been easy. I have experienced numerous narrow spots, the list of which will not be shared with you in this book. My narrow spots have been positive and negative, large and small, have included crisis and disaster and have occurred by accident and design. And in my response to them, I have stumbled as often as I have succeeded. I do not profess to have "the answers" for myself or for anyone else. Life is challenging—even downright messy sometimes! The challenge for each of us is to find within ourselves the authenticity to follow our unique life path, no matter where it goes.

THIS IS MORE
THAN A BOOK ABOUT CANCER.

In 2003, I was a left-handed woman.

I was also a wife and mother, in apparent good health.

Then my life journey changed unexpectedly, due to a cancer diagnosis. Since that time, I have developed a dramatically different perspective on life, reflecting on the lessons learned after moving through what I have come to call "the narrow spots." I now believe cancer to be an extraordinarily powerful and proficient teacher offering the potential for profound transformation.

This is more than a book about cancer. I want to empower you to live life resiliently, no matter what challenges you face. I hope you are inspired by the story you read here.

It all started in January of 2003, when I noticed a small lump on my left wrist. I wasn't worried, but I knew the bump was not normal. I did not think about cancer.

In 1991, my sister Kristin had had a reoccurrence of malignant melanoma that metastasized into her lungs and brain. She died before her thirty-sixth birthday, leaving behind her husband and two small boys, not to mention me and all the other people who loved her. At that time, for me, cancer was evil.

When the doctor showed me the MRI of my lump, it looked like a 6-inch mortadella sausage was growing in my hand, wrist and forearm. After a biopsy he said, "It is sarcoma."

Tears ran down my cheeks.

At home, I did a little Internet research, googling the word "sarcoma." I read that amputation is part of the treatment in at least 15% of cases. That was as far as I read.

At dinner with two good friends, I told them about the cancer, including the part about amputation. I said I would not accept the amputation of my dominant, left hand. I would do whatever treatment was necessary, but I would not, could not choose to lose my hand.

I wanted to LIVE.

When the doctor explained the treatment package, he said first would come chemotherapy and then surgery to remove the tumor. He and I both knew the tumor filled my wrist. So, I cut to the chase and asked, "What will happen if I do not accept amputation?"

His response was, "You will die."

I asked him, "If I were your wife or mother, what would you want me to do?"

He answered, "The difficult thing."

I wanted to live. And so, I bargained, "Couldn't I offer both of my breasts?" The doctor smiled. He knew that I was saying "Yes" to amputation and "Yes" to life.

Cancer was THE NARROW SPOT IN AN HOURGLASS and I was the sand.

Making that treatment decision meant accepting the unimaginable—something that was life-altering, disfiguring, potentially lifesaving, and with no guarantees. Embracing the reality of amputation, and the choices afforded me with that reality, I needed to reframe my life. I needed to change my perspective.

Spending time in solitude, prayer and meditation—moving from my head to my heart—helped me to say "Yes." I would have a change in my physical body, but my heart knew that I would move forward and grow through this experience with cancer.

For me, cancer was the narrow spot in an hourglass and I was the sand. I would travel down, through the tight spot, arriving at the bottom; the same sand, but with a different arrangement.

Narrow spots—the bumps, potholes and detours on the road of life—represent loss of one kind or another, require conscious acknowledgement and grieving, and are often accompanied by fear. Fear keeps us from being open and moving forward. It does not prevent us from experiencing narrow spots; it only makes it more difficult to pass through. We can go kicking and screaming, but we will go! The secret is not to fight the passage, but to bravely accept what is—to say, "Yes"—and embrace the passage; not a stoic surrender, rather a courageous reconciliation with reality. This "Yes" is certainly easier said than done.

Poet Rainer Marie Rilke wrote: *Be patient toward all that is unsolved in your heart and try to love the questions themselves.... Do not seek the answers, which cannot be given you, because you would not be able to live them. And the point is, to live everything. Live the questions now. And perhaps someday, far in the future, without even knowing it, you will live your way into the answers.*

We give and accept answers too quickly, seek to take away emotional pain too easily, and too often distract ourselves with busyness, often before we have learned what the narrow spot has to teach us. We must learn how to rest at the bottom of the hourglass, without answers, without conclusions, and, some days, without meaning.

Poet Stephen Levine writes, "It is an insistent grace that draws us / to the edge and beckons us surrender / safe territory and enter our enormity."

From the point of deciding to "surrender safe territory," things moved quickly—like going over a high waterfall with a child's inner tube. I enlisted friends and family to be my support team and had a "Name that Tumor" contest. The winner was "Goliath," the seemingly unbeatable foe defeated by a neophyte trusting in God.

I EMPOWERED MYSELF

TO MAKE THAT CHOICE.

Ten days after treatment began, I lost my hair, right on cue. Even though I had purchased an expensive wig and had my stylist work on it, I could not wear it. I did not recognize myself in the mirror. Instead I learned to creatively tie beautiful scarves to cover my bald head. I empowered myself to make that choice.

However, the chemo was having no affect on the tumor. It was growing.

On Friday, June 13, 2003, I had surgery to remove the lower part of my dominant left arm.

It reminds me to
Live every day.

Two months later my daughter Anna's wedding took place, a significant event on so many levels. I was very happy to be there, wearing a dress designed to minimize notice of my one-handedness. It was a glorious day—a celebration of life and love.

Cancer dwells as an ever-present shadow on my life. It reminds me to live every day. I am grateful for that awareness.

WE DO NOT NEED TO
WAIT FOR SICKNESS TO
SEEK WELLNESS.

When I reflect on my healing journey, I am keenly aware of the difference between the word "cure", the absence of disease, and the word "healing", wellness; becoming sound or healthy. We all know people who are disease free, but not well in body, mind and spirit.

In 1948, the year I was born, the World Health Organization stated, "Health is a state of complete physical, mental and social well-being, and not merely the absence of disease or infirmity." We do not need to wait for sickness to seek wellness.

I am a woman of FAITH.

The root definition of the word *health* is "whole." I am most definitely whole, even though I have a gaping hole in my silhouette. I am whole because I have come to understand that wholeness resides inside. It requires being patient with myself and present with God. I am a woman of faith. When narrow spots occur, I "pray as if it all depends on God and work as if it all depends on me," to quote St. Augustine.

YOU HAVE THE RESOURCES
WITH WHICH TO FACE
LIFE'S NARROW SPOTS.

A healing journey has many paths—as unique as the individual on that path. My fervent prayer for us all is to be well. You rarely get to choose your narrow spots; but you do get to choose what you take with you on the passage. You have the resources with which to face life's narrow spots. They are there in the sand in the hourglass. Find them. Sift them out. Sooner rather than later.

Have the courage to choose to accept—to say, "Yes"—to whatever narrow spots come your way. Embrace the passage and navigate, with intention and your unique well of resources, on the ever-changing journey called life.

DON'T JUST GO THROUGH THE NARROW SPOTS,
GROW THROUGH THEM.

The hourglass sand is important to my message. Sand is irritating, an abrasive. Even a tiny amount irritates when it is present in an unexpected way or place. The root definition of the word *inspire* is, "to breathe into." I invite you to breathe in even one grain of sand from this book, and allow it to provide some irritation to an attitude that you might hold about your life circumstance, healing, change and even cancer. We all know what happens to the oyster when sand gets into it.
It grows a pearl.

Don't just go through the narrow spots, grow through them.

My String of Pearls

PRACTICE PATIENCE: Have patience with yourself and your narrow spot. Patience is not waiting passively while someone else does something, nor is it stubborn endurance. It is an honest, gentle relationship with yourself.

PRACTICE PRESENCE: *BE* where you are. Presence requires slowing down, breathing deeply and listening to your heart. The root definition of the word *enthusiasm* is "inspired by God." I have found that presence is a necessary component to experiencing this inspiration.

HAVE FAITH: Any circumstance in life, no matter how challenging it appears, if responded to in faith, can be transformed. Faith does not entitle us to any exemption from narrow spots. Faith confronts the fear and gives us courage and confidence for the passage through them.

BE UPHELD BY A COMMUNITY OF SUPPORT: Being held up in a net of support, care, concern and prayer is palpable and powerful. Asking for help is a gift to the other person as well as a gift to you. Surround yourself with the abundance found in community.

MAKE THE INTENTION TO BE WHOLE: Intention requires effort and commitment—not perfection. Deciding to pay attention to what is happening and being present opens us up to move forward in faith with wholehearted confidence. We set the course for our journey and then travel with the courage and assurance that we will end up where we need to be, even though it may not be where we thought we would be.

MAINTAIN A SENSE OF HUMOR: There is very little that is funny about narrow spots. However, maintaining a sense of humor has helped me and those in my community of support to stay engaged in the journey.

EXPRESS GRATITUDE: People who come to recognize the benefit of navigating narrow spots with patience, presence, faith, intention, humor and community find expressing gratitude to be the beginning of giving back.

BE OPEN TO GRACE: Narrow spots are tools that provide us with life lessons that lead us to compassion and wisdom. Pay attention. The rest is grace, freely given, ever present and always in our favor. Grace has nothing to do with worthiness. It has everything to do with trust and surrender.

RUTH BACHMAN is a native of and still resides in Minnesota. In addition to being a wife, mother and grandmother, she is an author, educator, speaker and cancer advocate. Since 1992, her purpose statement has been, "to share my enthusiasm with the world."

This guiding principle has provided Ruth the opportunity to contribute her time, her resources and her talents in a number of roles; and to discover skills, attitudes and perspectives that are essential to navigating change, the one constant in life.

WITH GRATITUDE

My gratitude goes out to the many who have helped me achieve my goal of thriving after facing my narrow spots. Life has taught me that we don't get anywhere without the support of a community of caring people. While naming all the individuals would be impossible, I want to highlight my family: Dale, Bryan and Jessica, Anna and David, and my three wonderful grandchildren, Amy, Joel and Tatum; and dear friends: Stephanie Ross, Diane Brady and Guido Fratini.

BOOK PROCEEDS

Out of a deep sense of gratitude, Ruth donates proceeds from this book to support cancer education, advocacy and research.

THE HOURGLASS FUND PROJECT

Healing is synonymous with wholeness of body, mind and spirit. The Hourglass Fund Project (THFP) was established to support the Hourglass Fund at the Minnesota Medical Foundation, University of Minnesota,and Rein in Sarcoma (RIS). The Hourglass Fund fosters collaboration between the Masonic Cancer Center and the Center for Spirituality & Healing, both at the University of Minnesota, and to support research projects that explore the intersection between cancer and integrative healing practices. Support for RIS is to foster greater awareness about sarcoma and to support all of their essential programs. Support from THFP provides others with the opportunity to choose life and live it fully as they are passing through the narrow spot called cancer.

TO FIND OUT MORE, PLEASE GO TO WWW.RUTHBACHMAN.COM